The Essential Guide to Leadership: Practical Strategies and Tools for Effective Leadership

I0479934

By Mark Lowe

Acknowledgements:

I would like to express my heartfelt gratitude to my wife, Annie, for her unwavering support, encouragement, and understanding throughout the entire process of writing this book. Her patience and dedication have been instrumental in making this book a reality.

I also want to acknowledge my father, whose teachings and guidance laid the foundation for my leadership journey. His wisdom and inspiration have been a constant source of motivation and encouragement.

To the great leaders who have mentored me throughout my career, I extend my deepest appreciation. Your guidance and expertise have been invaluable, and I am forever grateful for the knowledge and insights you have shared.

Finally, I would like to express my sincere thanks to the readers of this book. It is my hope that the strategies and techniques presented in these pages will inspire and empower you to become the best leader you can be, and to make a positive impact in your own lives and the lives of those around you.

Preface

- Explanation of the importance of leadership skills

Chapter 1: Understanding Yourself as a Leader

- Identifying your leadership style and strengths
- Assessing your weaknesses and areas for improvement
- Developing self-awareness as a leader

Chapter 2: Developing a Vision

- Defining a clear and compelling vision for your team or organization
- Communicating your vision effectively to others
- Aligning your team with your vision

Chapter 3: Building Relationships and Communicating Effectively

- Building strong relationships with your team and stakeholders
- Effective communication techniques for leaders
- Active listening and understanding others' perspectives

Chapter 4: Motivating and Inspiring Your Team

- Understanding what motivates your team
- Techniques for inspiring and energizing your team
- Creating a positive and supportive work environment

Chapter 5: Developing and Empowering Your Team

- Identifying and developing talent within your team
- Delegating effectively
- Providing feedback and coaching for growth

Chapter 6: Leading Through Change and Adversity

- Strategies for leading through change

- Managing conflict and difficult situations

- Overcoming obstacles and adversity

Chapter 7: Continuous Improvement and Learning

- Embracing a growth mindset as a leader

- Identifying areas for personal and professional growth

- Creating a culture of learning and development within your team or organization

Conclusion

- Recap of key takeaways and lessons learned

- Final thoughts and encouragement for readers to continue developing their leadership skills.

Preface

Enron was an energy company that became one of the largest corporations in the United States during the 1990s. However, in the early 2000s, the company's unethical practices and poor leadership led to its ultimate demise.

Enron's leadership, including CEO Jeffrey Skilling and Chairman Kenneth Lay, were known for their aggressive business tactics and focus on short-term profits. They encouraged employees to take risks and engage in accounting fraud in order to make the company's financials appear stronger than they actually were. This ultimately led to Enron's bankruptcy in 2001, and the company's stock price fell from over $90 per share to less than $1.

The Enron scandal was a cautionary tale about the importance of ethical leadership and the dangers of focusing solely on short-term profits. Enron's leaders were more concerned with their own financial gains than the well-being of the company and its employees. The scandal led to increased government regulation of the financial industry and a greater emphasis on corporate responsibility and transparency.

The Enron case serves as a reminder that strong leadership is essential for the success of any organization. Leaders must prioritize ethical behavior, focus on long-term goals, and create a culture of transparency and accountability. Failure to do so can have serious consequences for the company and its stakeholders.

Leadership skills are essential not just for those in positions of authority, but for anyone looking to make a positive impact in their personal and professional lives. Good leadership can inspire and motivate others, foster a positive work environment, and drive progress towards common goals. However, becoming a better leader is not an easy task, and it requires dedication and continuous improvement.

This book is designed to provide readers with the tools and knowledge they need to become better leaders. Whether you are a seasoned executive, a new manager, or an aspiring leader, the principles and strategies outlined in this book will help you develop the skills necessary to lead with excellence.

Through a combination of practical advice, real-world examples, and insightful analysis, this book will guide you on a journey of self-discovery and growth. You will learn how to understand yourself as a leader, develop a clear vision for your team, build strong relationships, motivate, and inspire others, and lead through change and adversity.

By the end of this book, you will be equipped with the knowledge and skills necessary to lead with excellence and make a positive impact in your organization and community.

Dear reader,

Before you begin diving into this book on leadership, I challenge you to take a moment to reflect on your current approach to leadership. Consider the values that drive you, the strengths, and weaknesses you possess, and the areas in which you hope to improve. Be honest with yourself about the challenges you face and the obstacles that have held you back.

Now, I challenge you to approach this book with an open mind and a willingness to learn. As you read, take note of the insights and advice shared by the various leaders and experts presented. Consider how you might apply these lessons to your own leadership style, and be willing to try new approaches and experiment with new strategies.

Most importantly, I challenge you to commit to ongoing growth and development as a leader. Leadership is a journey, not a destination, and there is always room to improve. Embrace the challenges and opportunities that lie ahead and take concrete steps to become the best leader you can be.

I wish you all the best in your leadership journey, and I hope this book proves to be a valuable resource on your path to success.

Sincerely,

Mark

Chapter 1:

Understanding Yourself as a Leader

"To lead others, you must first lead yourself - and to lead yourself, you must first understand yourself."

Howard Schultz, the former CEO of Starbucks. Schultz is known for his innovative leadership style and his ability to create a strong company culture. One of the keys to his success was his deep understanding of himself as a leader.

Early in his career, Schultz worked for a small coffee shop in Seattle called Starbucks. He was impressed by the quality of the coffee and the passion of the employees, but he felt that the company had lost its way. He believed that Starbucks had lost sight of its original mission - to create a third place between work and home where people could relax and connect with each other.

Schultz left Starbucks to start his own coffee company, Il Giornale. However, he soon realized that he missed the community and culture of Starbucks. He decided to buy the company and become its CEO.

As CEO, Schultz focused on creating a strong company culture that reflected his own values and vision. He believed that the key to success was to create a company that was focused on people - both employees and customers. He implemented policies that reflected this, such as providing health insurance and stock options to all employees and creating a welcoming environment in every Starbucks location.

Schultz's understanding of himself as a leader allowed him to create a company culture that was true to his values and vision. He was able to create a company that was not only successful financially but also made a positive impact on the world. Starbucks became known as a company that cared about its employees, its customers, and the communities where it operated.

Schultz's story is an example of how understanding yourself as a leader is essential for success. By understanding his own values and vision,

Schultz was able to create a company culture that reflected those values and ultimately led to the success of Starbucks.

Identifying your leadership style and strengths

Identifying your leadership style and strengths is an essential part of becoming an effective leader. Knowing your leadership style and strengths allows you to play to your strengths and lead in a way that is authentic and effective.

One way to identify your leadership style is to reflect on your past experiences as a leader. Think about the situations in which you have been most effective as a leader and what strategies you used to achieve success. Consider the feedback you have received from others about your leadership style.

Another way to identify your leadership style is to take a leadership assessment or personality test. These tools can provide insight into your personality traits, leadership style, and strengths.

Once you have identified your leadership style, it is important to focus on your strengths as a leader. Your strengths are the skills and abilities that come naturally to you and that you excel at. By focusing on your strengths, you can maximize your effectiveness as a leader and create a positive impact on those around you.

Identifying your leadership style and strengths is an ongoing process that requires self-reflection and feedback from others. As you continue to develop as a leader, it is important to stay attuned to your strengths and weaknesses and to adjust your leadership style accordingly. With a strong understanding of your leadership style and strengths, you can become a more effective and successful leader.

Below is a quick self-assessment. Be honest with yourself and look for opportunities to grow.

Leadership Assessment:

1. How well do you communicate with others? a. Excellent - 5 points b. Good - 4 points c. Average - 3 points d. Below average - 2 points e. Poor - 1 point

2. How do you handle conflicts with others? a. Effectively resolve conflicts - 5 points b. Mostly resolve conflicts - 4 points c. Somewhat resolve conflicts - 3 points d. Rarely resolve conflicts - 2 points e. Unable to resolve conflicts - 1 point

3. How well do you empower and delegate tasks to your team members? a. Always empower and delegate tasks - 5 points b. Mostly empower and delegate tasks - 4 points c. Sometimes empower and delegate tasks - 3 points d. Rarely empower and delegate tasks - 2 points e. Never empower and delegate tasks - 1 point

4. How do you handle stressful situations? a. Remain calm and focused - 5 points b. Mostly remain calm and focused - 4 points c. Sometimes become anxious or stressed - 3 points d. Frequently become anxious or stressed - 2 points e. Always become anxious or stressed - 1 point

5. How well do you collaborate with others? a. Excellent collaborator - 5 points b. Good collaborator - 4 points c. Average collaborator - 3 points d. Poor collaborator - 2 points e. Unable to collaborate - 1 point

Grading Key: 20-25 points - Excellent leadership skills 15-19 points - good leadership skills 10-14 points - Average leadership skills 5-9 points - Below average leadership skills 1-4 points - Poor leadership skills

Note: This is a simplified leadership assessment and is not intended to be used as a comprehensive evaluation tool. It is recommended to seek the advice of a professional leadership coach or consultant for a more thorough assessment.

Assessing your weaknesses and areas for improvement

Assessing your weaknesses and areas for improvement is a crucial step in becoming a better leader. While every leader has strengths, no one is perfect, and even the most successful leaders have areas in which they can improve.

One way to assess your weaknesses is to seek feedback from others. Ask your colleagues, team members, or mentors for constructive feedback about your leadership style, communication skills, and areas where they believe you could improve. It is important to listen actively and avoid becoming defensive when receiving feedback. Instead, use the feedback to identify areas where you can improve and develop a plan to address them.

Another way to assess your weaknesses is to reflect on your own experiences as a leader. Consider situations where you felt challenged or struggled to lead effectively and think about what you could have done differently to achieve a better outcome. Self-reflection can be difficult, but it is an essential part of personal growth and development.

Once you have identified your weaknesses and areas for improvement, it is important to develop a plan to address them. This could involve seeking additional training or mentorship, practicing new communication or leadership strategies, or delegating tasks to others who are better suited for certain responsibilities. It is essential to be patient with yourself as you work on improving your weaknesses. Change takes time, and it is normal to experience setbacks along the way. However, with dedication and perseverance, you can overcome your weaknesses and become a more effective leader.

Assessing your weaknesses and areas for improvement is an ongoing process that requires self-reflection, feedback from others, and a willingness to learn and grow. By identifying your weaknesses and developing a plan to address them, you can become a more effective and successful leader. Remember, nobody is perfect, but with dedication and hard work, you can continue to improve and achieve your leadership goals.

Satya Nadella, the current CEO of Microsoft, is a well-known example of a leader who recognized and improved upon his weaknesses. When Nadella first took on the role in 2014, he faced criticism for his lack of experience in leading a large corporation.

To address this weakness, Nadella sought feedback from his colleagues and team members. He recognized the importance of getting input from others to improve his leadership skills and make better decisions for the company. He regularly held one-on-one meetings with his employees to discuss their ideas and concerns and participated in group discussions and forums to hear feedback from a wider range of perspectives.

Nadella also worked with executive coaches to develop his communication and leadership strategies. He recognized that effective communication was crucial to being a successful leader and worked to improve his public speaking, writing, and presentation skills. Nadella also emphasized empathy and inclusivity in his leadership style, which helped to improve the company culture at Microsoft and promote collaboration among employees.

Nadella's commitment to self-improvement and his willingness to seek feedback from others has been a key factor in his success as a leader. Under his leadership, Microsoft has seen significant growth and success, with the company's market value more than doubling since he took on the role of CEO. Nadella's example serves as a reminder that no leader is perfect, but with a willingness to learn and grow, it is possible to overcome weaknesses and achieve great success.

In short, if you want to be a great leader, you must accept you have weaknesses and you must commit to continuous improvement.

In an interview with Harvard Business Review, Oprah Winfrey discussed her journey towards becoming a more self-aware and effective leader.

Winfrey revealed that she used to be a micromanager, always trying to control every aspect of her business and personal life. However, as she started to achieve more success, she realized that this approach was limiting her growth and potential as a leader. She began to engage in self-reflection to identify her weaknesses and areas for improvement.

Winfrey took time to reflect on her own behavior and motivations and worked to understand how her past experiences and beliefs were influencing her leadership style. She also sought feedback from her colleagues and team members, and actively listened to their perspectives on her leadership style.

Through this process of self-reflection and feedback, Winfrey was able to develop a more collaborative and empowering leadership style. She learned to trust her team members and delegate tasks to them, and to focus on building a culture of trust and respect within her organization.

Overall, Winfrey's commitment to self-reflection and self-awareness has helped her become a more effective and successful leader and has enabled her to build a thriving media empire. Her example demonstrates the importance of engaging in regular self-reflection to identify your weaknesses and areas for improvement, and to develop a leadership style that is grounded in collaboration, trust, and empathy.

Developing self-awareness as a leader requires engaging in regular self-reflection. Self-reflection involves taking time to examine your own thoughts, feelings, and actions in different situations. This process can help you gain a better understanding of your own emotions, values, and biases, as well as how they may influence your decision-making and interactions with others.

To engage in self-reflection, set aside regular time to reflect on your own behavior and reactions in different situations. Consider how your emotions and biases may have impacted your interactions with others and reflect on the outcomes of these interactions. You can also reflect on your own values and beliefs, and how they may shape your leadership style and decision-making.

Another way to engage in self-reflection is to keep a journal or diary. This can be a useful tool for tracking your thoughts and emotions over time and identifying patterns in your behavior and decision-making. Reviewing your journal entries regularly can help you gain insights into your own behavior and emotions and identify areas where you may need to make changes or improvements.

Self-reflection requires a willingness to be honest and open with yourself, and to examine your own behavior and motivations objectively. It can be a challenging process, but it is an important part of developing self-awareness as a leader. By engaging in regular self-reflection, you can gain a better understanding of your own strengths and weaknesses as a leader and develop strategies to address areas where you may need to improve.

Self-reflection is a critical component of developing self-awareness as a leader. By taking time to reflect on your own behavior, emotions, and values, you can gain insights into your own decision-making and interactions with others. This can help you become a more effective and successful leader, and better serve the needs of your team and organization. Remember, self-reflection requires ongoing effort and dedication, but it is a powerful tool for personal and professional growth.

Questions to Ponder

What are some of the qualities that you admire in great leaders?

How do you embody those qualities in your own leadership style?

What are some areas where you can improve?

Chapter 2:

Developing a Vision

"Without a clear vision, a leader becomes a wanderer, but with a vision, they become a pathfinder."

Steve Jobs, the co-founder, and former CEO of Apple. Jobs was known for his ability to create compelling visions that inspired his team members and customers alike.

In the early 2000s, Apple was facing declining sales and a lack of innovation. Jobs returned to the company and quickly set about developing a new vision for the organization. He recognized that Apple needed to focus on creating innovative products that combined technology with design, and that would appeal to a wide range of consumers.

Jobs developed a clear and compelling vision for Apple's future that was centered around the company's core strengths and values. He focused on creating a product ecosystem that seamlessly integrated hardware, software, and services, and that provided a user experience that was intuitive and elegant.

Jobs communicated this vision to his team members and stakeholders through a series of highly anticipated product launches, including the iPod, iPhone, and iPad. These products embodied Apple's vision of creating beautiful and innovative products that were easy to use and seamlessly integrated into people's lives.

Under Jobs' leadership, Apple experienced a period of unprecedented growth and success, with the company becoming one of the most valuable in the world. Jobs' ability to provide a clear and compelling vision for Apple's future was a key factor in the company's success, and his example demonstrates the importance of developing a strong vision for any organization.

Defining a clear and compelling vision is a critical aspect of effective leadership. A vision serves as a roadmap for the future, providing direction and purpose for the team or organization. It outlines where the organization is going and what it aims to achieve and helps to align team members around a shared set of goals and objectives.

To develop a clear and compelling vision, leaders must first take time to reflect on the core values and purpose of the organization. They should consider the organization's strengths and weaknesses and identify areas where they can leverage their unique strengths to achieve their goals. They should also consider the external environment, such as market trends and competitor activities, and how these may impact the organization's future.

Once these factors have been considered, leaders can begin to develop a vision statement that encapsulates the organization's core purpose and goals. A good vision statement should be clear, concise, and inspiring, and should capture the imagination of team members and stakeholders.

To ensure that the vision is compelling and resonates with team members, leaders should involve their team members in the process of developing the vision. They should solicit feedback and ideas from team members and work collaboratively to develop a shared understanding of the organization's purpose and goals.

Finally, it's important to communicate the vision clearly and consistently to team members and stakeholders. Leaders should use a variety of communication channels, such as email, social media, and in-person meetings, to ensure that the vision is widely understood and embraced. They should also use the vision as a guiding principle in decision-making and ensure that all team members are aligned around the vision and working towards its achievement.

Developing a clear and compelling vision is an essential aspect of effective leadership. It provides direction and purpose for the organization, aligns team members around a shared set of goals, and serves as a guiding principle for decision-making. By taking the time to develop a strong vision statement, involving team members in the process, and communicating the vision clearly and consistently, leaders can create a strong foundation for success and ensure that their organization achieves its full potential.

Communicating your vision effectively to others

Developing a clear and compelling vision for your organization is just the first step in effective leadership. To ensure that your vision is realized, you must also be able to communicate it effectively to others.

Communicating your vision effectively requires a multi-faceted approach. First, it's important to use clear and concise language to articulate your vision. Avoid using jargon or technical terms that may be unfamiliar to your team members or stakeholders, and instead use simple, easy-to-understand language that resonates with your audience.

It's also important to use a variety of communication channels to ensure that your vision is communicated to as many people as possible. This may include email, social media, in-person meetings, presentations, or other forms of communication.

Another key aspect of communicating your vision effectively is to personalize it for your audience. Consider the interests and motivations of your team members and stakeholders, and tailor your messaging to appeal to their specific needs and goals. This will help to ensure that your vision is relevant and meaningful to everyone who hears it.

Finally, it's important to follow up on your vision with actions. Your team members and stakeholders will be looking to you to demonstrate your commitment to the vision, and to provide guidance and support as they work towards achieving it. By taking an active role in implementing the vision, you will demonstrate your leadership and inspire others to follow your lead.

Communicating your vision effectively is a critical aspect of effective leadership. By using clear language, a variety of communication channels, personalizing your messaging, and following up with action, you can ensure that your vision is embraced by your team members and stakeholders, and that your organization is set up for success.

Aligning your team with your vision

To achieve success, it's not enough to simply have a vision - you must also align your team with it.

Take Steve Jobs, for example. Jobs had a clear and compelling vision for Apple - to create innovative and beautifully designed products that would change the world. To align his team with this vision, Jobs was known for his rigorous attention to detail, his passion for design, and his relentless pursuit of excellence.

One way Jobs aligned his team with his vision was by setting clear and specific goals that were directly tied to the vision. For example, he set the goal of creating the first personal computer with a graphical user interface, which eventually led to the creation of the Macintosh computer. He also set the goal of creating the first digital music player that was easy to use and beautifully designed, which led to the creation of the iPod.

Jobs also created a culture that supported his vision by establishing a set of values that were aligned with it. He emphasized the importance of design, simplicity, and innovation, and encouraged his team members to embody these values in their work. He also celebrated successes and recognized team members who demonstrated these values, which helped to reinforce the culture and build a sense of shared purpose.

Finally, Jobs provided ongoing support and guidance to his team members as they worked towards achieving the vision. He was known for his hands-on approach and his willingness to get involved in every aspect of the business, from product design to marketing to customer service. He provided feedback and coaching to his team members and ensured that they had the tools and support they needed to succeed.

By aligning his team with his vision in these ways, Steve Jobs was able to create a company that has had a profound impact on the world of technology and design, and that continues to innovate and push the boundaries of what is possible.

Aligning your team with your vision involves several key steps. The first step is to ensure that your team members understand your vision and are committed to it. This may involve communicating your vision effectively (as discussed in the previous section), but it may also require additional efforts, such as team meetings, training sessions, or one-on-one conversations.

Once your team members understand your vision, the next step is to align their goals and objectives with it. This may involve setting clear and specific goals that are directly tied to the vision and ensuring that each team member understands how their work contributes to the overall success of the organization.

Another key aspect of aligning your team with your vision is to create a culture that supports the vision. This may involve establishing a set of values that are aligned with the vision and encouraging team members to demonstrate these values in their work. It may also involve celebrating successes and recognizing team members who embody the vision and values of the organization.

Finally, it's important to provide ongoing support and guidance to your team members as they work towards achieving the vision. This may involve providing training and resources, offering feedback, and coaching, and ensuring that team members have the tools and support they need to succeed.

Aligning your team with your vision is a critical aspect of effective leadership. By ensuring that your team members understand and are committed to the vision, aligning their goals and objectives with it, creating a culture that supports the vision, and providing ongoing support and guidance, you can set your organization up for success and achieve your vision together.

Questions to Ponder

What is your leadership philosophy?

How does it inform your decision-making as a leader?

How do you communicate your philosophy to your team?

Chapter 3:

Building Relationships and Communicating Effectively

"Communication builds relationships; relationships build trust; trust drives success."

Indra Nooyi, the former CEO of PepsiCo. During her tenure, Nooyi implemented several initiatives aimed at building a strong team culture and fostering positive relationships with stakeholders.

One of the key initiatives that Nooyi implemented was the "Performance with Purpose" program, which was aimed at making PepsiCo a more socially and environmentally responsible company. This program helped to build trust with stakeholders by demonstrating PepsiCo's commitment to sustainability and ethical business practices.

Nooyi also worked hard to build strong relationships with her team members. She implemented a "360-degree feedback" program, which allowed team members to give and receive feedback from one another. This program helped to build trust and transparency within the team and allowed for constructive feedback and collaboration.

In addition, Nooyi was known for her personal touch when it came to building relationships with team members. She took the time to get to know team members personally and showed genuine interest in their lives and careers. She also made herself available to team members and encouraged them to come to her with any questions or concerns.

Through these initiatives, Nooyi was able to build a strong team culture and positive relationships with stakeholders. This helped to drive success for PepsiCo, and cemented Nooyi's reputation as a successful and effective leader.

Building strong relationships with your team and stakeholders is crucial for effective leadership. Here are some key steps you can take:

- Listen actively: Listen to your team members and stakeholders with an open mind and be willing to consider their perspectives and ideas.

- Communicate clearly: Communicate your expectations, goals, and vision clearly and regularly to ensure that everyone is on the same page.

- Show empathy: Show empathy and understanding towards team members and stakeholders and be sensitive to their needs and concerns.

- Foster a positive team culture: Foster a positive team culture that encourages collaboration, creativity, and innovation.

- Recognize achievements: Recognize and celebrate team members' achievements and show appreciation for their contributions.

- Build trust: Build trust with your team members and stakeholders by being honest, transparent, and accountable.

- Be available: Be available to your team members and stakeholders, and make sure they feel comfortable coming to you with questions or concerns.

By taking these steps, you can build strong relationships with your team members and stakeholders, which will help you achieve your goals and drive success.

Leaders who build strong relationships with their team members and stakeholders are more likely to achieve their goals and drive success. Strong relationships foster trust, collaboration, and innovation, and help to create a positive team culture. When team members and stakeholders feel valued and supported, they are more likely to be engaged and committed to the organization's goals. In addition, strong relationships can help leaders to navigate challenges and obstacles more effectively, as they have a network of trusted advisors and supporters to rely on. By prioritizing relationship-building, leaders can create a more resilient and effective organization that is better equipped to tackle complex problems and achieve long-term success.

Effective communication techniques for leaders

Blockbuster was once a dominant force in the home video rental market, with over 9,000 stores worldwide. However, the company failed to adapt to changing consumer preferences and the rise of digital streaming, and eventually filed for bankruptcy in 2010.

One of the key reasons for Blockbuster's downfall was its leadership's failure to build strong relationships with its employees and customers, and to communicate effectively with them. For example, the company's managers were known for their strict adherence to policies and procedures, rather than working collaboratively with employees to solve problems and improve customer service.

Blockbuster also failed to effectively communicate its value proposition to customers, which resulted in a decline in customer loyalty and ultimately contributed to its downfall. The company was slow to adapt to changing consumer preferences and the rise of digital streaming and failed to effectively communicate its vision and strategy to stakeholders.

We can learn from this example is the importance of leaders building strong relationships with their team members and stakeholders and communicating effectively with them. Leaders who fail to do so risk losing the trust and loyalty of their employees and customers and may struggle to adapt to changing market conditions.

Effective communication is a critical skill for leaders, as it allows them to convey their vision, build relationships, and drive success. Some key communication techniques that leaders can use include active listening, clear and concise messaging, and adapting communication styles to suit different audiences.

Active listening involves paying close attention to what others are saying and responding in a way that demonstrates understanding and empathy. This can help leaders to build trust and rapport with team members and stakeholders and ensure that they are able to address concerns or questions effectively.

Clear and concise messaging is also important for effective communication. Leaders should strive to articulate their vision and goals in a way that is easy to understand and memorable. Using simple and direct language, avoiding jargon, and focusing on key messages can help to ensure that communication is effective and impactful.

Leaders should be able to adapt their communication style to suit different audiences. This means tailoring communication to the needs, preferences, and cultural backgrounds of team members and stakeholders. By taking the time to understand and adapt to different communication styles, leaders can build stronger relationships and achieve better outcomes.

Active listening and understanding others' perspectives

Active listening and understanding others' perspectives are crucial skills for leaders to develop. These skills allow leaders to connect with their team members and stakeholders, build trust, and create a more inclusive and collaborative work environment.

Active listening involves fully concentrating on what the other person is saying, without interrupting or making assumptions. Leaders can demonstrate active listening by asking open-ended questions, clarifying what the other person is saying, and summarizing their thoughts and feelings.

Understanding others' perspectives goes beyond simply listening to what they are saying. It requires empathy and the ability to put oneself in another person's shoes. Leaders who understand others' perspectives are better equipped to address their concerns, provide support, and create solutions that work for everyone.

By developing active listening and understanding others' perspectives, leaders can foster a culture of open communication and collaboration, which can lead to improved team performance, higher employee engagement, and increased stakeholder satisfaction.

Here's an assessment on active listening and understanding others' perspectives:

1. How often do you interrupt others while they are speaking? a. Almost always b. Sometimes c. Rarely d. Never

2. How often do you ask open-ended questions to understand others' perspectives? a. Almost never b. Sometimes c. Often d. Almost always

3. How often do you summarize what others have said to ensure understanding? a. Almost never b. Sometimes c. Often d. Almost always

4. How often do you consider other people's feelings and perspectives when making decisions? a. Almost never b. Sometimes c. Often d. Almost always

5. How often do you practice empathy in your interactions with others? a. Almost never b. Sometimes c. Often d. Almost always

Grading key:

- Mostly a's and b's: You may need to work on developing active listening and understanding others' perspectives. Consider seeking feedback from others and practicing mindfulness techniques to improve your listening skills.

- Mostly c's: You demonstrate some proficiency in active listening and understanding others' perspectives but may benefit from further practice and development.

- Mostly d's: You are highly skilled in active listening and understanding others' perspectives. Keep up the good work and continue to model these skills for others.

Questions to Ponder

What are some ways that you can build trust with your team?

How do you establish and maintain credibility as a leader?

What are some strategies for building relationships with team members?

Chapter 4:

Motivating and Inspiring Your Team

"A leader's ability to motivate and inspire their team determines the heights they can reach together."

Elon Musk is a leader who is well-known for his ability to motivate and inspire his teams. He is the CEO of Tesla, an electric car company, and SpaceX, a space exploration company. Musk has set ambitious goals for both companies, such as developing a fully electric car and making space travel more accessible. These goals may seem impossible, but Musk has been able to motivate and inspire his teams to achieve them.

One way Musk motivates his teams is by communicating his vision clearly. He often shares his goals and visions for the future with his employees, and he explains how each employee can contribute to achieving those goals. He also encourages his teams to think outside the box and come up with innovative solutions to problems. This approach fosters a culture of creativity and innovation within his teams, which helps to motivate employees to work hard towards achieving their goals.

In addition, Musk is a leader who leads by example. He is known for working long hours and being deeply involved in the day-to-day operations of both Tesla and SpaceX. By working alongside his employees, Musk shows that he is committed to achieving their goals and is willing to put in the hard work required to get there. This approach helps to inspire his employees to do the same.

Musk is also known for setting high expectations for his employees. He holds them accountable for their work and encourages them to take ownership of their projects. This approach helps to motivate employees to work harder and take pride in their work.

Elon Musk is a leader who can motivate and inspire his teams to achieve great things. By communicating his vision clearly, leading by example, and setting high expectations, Musk can create a culture of innovation and hard work within his teams. This approach has led to many impressive accomplishments, such as the development of the Tesla electric car and the successful launch of SpaceX's Falcon Heavy rocket.

Understanding what motivates your team

Understanding what motivates your team is crucial in being an effective leader. Motivation can come from a variety of sources, including financial incentives, recognition, personal fulfillment, and the desire for growth and development. As a leader, it's your responsibility to identify what motivates your team and create an environment that fosters motivation and engagement.

One effective way to identify what motivates your team is to get to know each member individually. Take the time to learn about their personal and professional goals, strengths, and challenges. This can be done through one-on-one meetings, performance evaluations, or informal conversations.

In addition to individual conversations, you can also conduct surveys or ask for feedback from your team to understand what drives them and what they find rewarding. Use this information to tailor your leadership approach to meet their individual needs and help them reach their full potential. For example, if you find that one team member is motivated by recognition, you can publicly acknowledge their achievements to provide a sense of accomplishment and motivation.

It's important to note that motivation can change over time, so regularly check in with your team to ensure that you are meeting their needs and keeping them engaged. By understanding what motivates your team and creating a supportive environment, you can foster a culture of motivation and inspire your team to achieve their goals.

Let's say you are a team leader for a software development company. You notice that one of your team members, John, has been consistently producing high-quality work and meeting his deadlines, but he doesn't seem to be as engaged in team meetings or social events as the other team members.

To understand what motivates John, you schedule a one-on-one meeting with him. During the meeting, you ask him about his personal and professional goals and what he enjoys about his work. You learn that John is motivated by the opportunity to work on challenging projects that allow him to use his creativity and problem-solving skills. He also values autonomy and the ability to work independently.

Armed with this information, you make a few changes to how you manage John. You assign him to work on a project that requires innovative problem-solving and give him the freedom to approach it in his own way. You also give him regular check-ins but allow him the space to work independently.

As a result, John becomes more engaged and motivated, producing even higher-quality work and sharing his ideas with the team more frequently. By taking the time to understand what motivates John and adapting your leadership style accordingly, you were able to increase his motivation and improve his performance, benefiting both John and the company.

Techniques for inspiring and energizing your team

As a leader, one of your most important responsibilities is to motivate and inspire your team. When team members are motivated and energized, they are more likely to be productive, engaged, and committed to achieving team goals. However, motivating and inspiring your team can be a challenging task, especially when team members have different personalities, motivations, and work styles. In this chapter, we will explore techniques for inspiring and energizing your team, including understanding what motivates your team, setting clear goals, celebrating successes, providing growth opportunities, fostering a positive work environment, and leading by example. By implementing these techniques, you can motivate and inspire your team to achieve their full potential and contribute to the success of your organization.

Here are some techniques for inspiring and energizing your team:

1. Set clear and challenging goals: Setting clear and challenging goals can motivate your team by giving them something to strive

for. Ensure that the goals are achievable but also challenging enough to inspire your team to work harder and achieve more.

2. Celebrate successes: Celebrate team successes by recognizing the efforts of individual team members and highlighting the team's achievements. This creates a positive and encouraging environment, which can motivate team members to continue working hard.

3. Provide opportunities for growth: Provide your team with opportunities for growth, such as training, mentoring, or stretch assignments. This shows your team that you are invested in their personal and professional development and can inspire them to work harder and achieve more.

4. Foster a positive work environment: Create a positive work environment by promoting open communication, collaboration, and respect among team members. This can improve team morale and foster a sense of camaraderie, which can energize and inspire your team.

5. Lead by example: Set a positive example for your team by exhibiting the behaviors and attitudes you want your team to emulate. This can inspire your team to follow your lead and work harder to achieve team goals.

By implementing these techniques, you can inspire and energize your team, leading to increased motivation, productivity, and overall performance.

For example, let's say you are a manager of a marketing team, and you have a team member, Sarah, who is very creative but lacks experience in data analysis. You recognize that in today's world of marketing, data analysis is a crucial skill that can help your team make better decisions and increase the effectiveness of your campaigns. Here are some techniques you could use to inspire and energize Sarah:

1. Provide opportunities for growth: You could enroll Sarah in a data analytics course or provide her with training on data

analysis tools and techniques. By providing her with these opportunities, you are investing in her development and showing that you value her as an individual contributor.

2. Set clear expectations: You could set clear expectations for Sarah's role in the team and provide her with a specific goal to work towards. For example, you could set a target for her to analyze the effectiveness of a specific marketing campaign using data analytics tools. By setting clear expectations, you can help Sarah focus her efforts and stay motivated.

3. Encourage collaboration: You could encourage Sarah to work closely with team members who are experienced in data analysis. By working together, Sarah can learn from their experience and gain new insights into data analysis techniques.

4. Provide recognition and rewards: When Sarah achieves her goal, you could recognize her achievement and reward her with something meaningful. This could be a bonus or promotion, but it could also be something more personalized, such as a gift card to her favorite restaurant or a day off. By providing recognition and rewards, you can motivate Sarah to continue developing her skills and contribute to the success of the team.

By using these techniques, you can help Sarah develop her data analysis skills, increase her effectiveness as a marketer, and ultimately benefit the team and the organization.

Creating a positive and supportive work environment

Creating a positive and supportive work environment is an essential component of effective leadership. A positive work environment can increase employee satisfaction, motivation, and productivity while reducing turnover rates and absenteeism. In contrast, a negative work environment can lead to employee burnout, low morale, and decreased job satisfaction.

One company that successfully created a positive and supportive work environment is Patagonia, an outdoor apparel and gear company.

Patagonia has a reputation for valuing sustainability, environmentalism, and employee well-being. The company has implemented several initiatives to create a positive work environment, such as offering on-site childcare, flexible work arrangements, and extensive employee benefits, including paid time off for environmental activism.

Patagonia also has a unique hiring process that focuses on cultural fit and values alignment rather than just skills and experience. They prioritize hiring individuals who share their values and beliefs, which helps to create a more cohesive and supportive team.

In addition, Patagonia encourages employee participation in company-wide decision-making and provides opportunities for career development and growth. The company's leadership also emphasizes transparency and open communication, which fosters trust and a sense of community among employees.

All these efforts have contributed to a positive and supportive work environment at Patagonia, which in turn has led to a highly engaged and motivated workforce. The company's commitment to its values and employees has also helped to attract and retain top talent, contributing to its success as a brand and a business.

One of the key elements of a positive work environment is trust. Leaders can build trust among team members by being transparent and honest, following through on promises, and giving credit where credit is due. When employees trust their leaders, they are more likely to take risks, share ideas, and collaborate openly.

Effective communication is another critical component of a positive work environment. Leaders should strive to create an environment that encourages open communication, active listening, and constructive feedback. Regular team meetings, one-on-one conversations, and employee surveys are all effective ways to gather feedback and address issues in a timely manner.

Collaboration and teamwork are also essential for a positive work environment. Leaders can foster collaboration by encouraging employees to work together on projects and creating cross-functional teams that bring together individuals with diverse skill sets and perspectives. By working together, employees can leverage their strengths, learn from each other, and achieve more significant results than they could alone.

Finally, leaders should support employees' personal and professional growth by offering opportunities for training, development, and advancement. This can include providing access to resources such as mentorship programs, leadership training, and tuition reimbursement.

By creating a positive and supportive work environment, leaders can help their teams thrive and achieve their full potential. This, in turn, can lead to increased productivity, employee satisfaction, and ultimately, organizational success.

Questions to Ponder

How do you create a vision for your team or organization?

How do you communicate that vision to your team and get them excited about it?

How do you measure progress toward your goals?

Chapter 5:

Developing and Empowering Your Team

"Empowerment is not giving power to your team, but rather unleashing the power within them."

In the 1990s, Gregg Popovich was an assistant coach for the San Antonio Spurs and was tasked with scouting international talent. During one of his trips to Europe, he discovered a young player named Tony Parker, who was only 15 years old at the time.

Popovich saw potential in Parker and convinced the Spurs to draft him in the first round of the 2001 NBA draft. Despite his youth and inexperience, Popovich recognized Parker's talent and worked with him to develop his skills. He empowered Parker to take on a bigger role on the team, allowing him to run the offense and become a team leader.

Under Popovich's guidance, Parker went on to become a six-time All-Star, four-time NBA champion, and the 2007 NBA Finals MVP. Popovich's ability to identify and develop talent within his team played a significant role in the Spurs' success during his tenure as head coach. This example shows that leaders who can recognize and nurture talent within their teams can achieve great success.

Identifying and developing talent within a team is a crucial aspect of leadership, as it helps to not only enhance the skills of individual team members but also contribute to the overall growth and success of the organization. To identify potential talent within the team, a leader must first assess the strengths and weaknesses of each team member through performance evaluations, feedback from other team members, and observing their work habits.

Once identified, the leader must provide opportunities for development and growth, such as providing additional training, mentoring, or assigning challenging projects to enhance their skills. A leader must also provide regular feedback to encourage progress and motivate team members to continue to develop and reach their full potential. A leader who effectively identifies and develops talent within the team not only strengthens the team's overall capabilities but also demonstrates a commitment to their team's success and growth.

Once you have identified the talent within your team, the next step is to develop and empower them. This involves providing them with the necessary training and resources to help them develop their skills and reach their full potential. One way to do this is through coaching and mentoring. As a leader, it is important to provide regular feedback and guidance to your team members, helping them to set clear goals and providing them with the support they need to achieve them.

Another way to develop talent within your team is by offering them challenging assignments and opportunities to take on new responsibilities. This can help to stretch their abilities and push them out of their comfort zones, allowing them to develop new skills and gain valuable experience. It is also important to recognize and reward your team members for their achievements, providing them with the recognition and incentives they need to stay motivated and engaged.

Overall, identifying and developing talent within your team is an essential part of effective leadership. By investing in your team members and providing them with the support and resources they need to grow and develop, you can create a more skilled and engaged workforce that is better equipped to meet the challenges of the future.

For example, let's say that you are a team leader at a marketing firm, and you want to assess the strengths and weaknesses of your team in order to identify areas for improvement and develop their talent. To do this, you could start by creating a list of the key skills and competencies required for success in your team's roles. This might include things like creativity, analytical thinking, project management, and communication skills.

Next, you can use a variety of methods to assess your team members' abilities in these areas. For example, you might review their past performance evaluations, speak with their colleagues and other stakeholders to get feedback on their strengths and weaknesses, or administer skills assessments or other tests.

Once you have identified areas where your team members could improve or develop their talent, you can create a plan for providing training, coaching, or other resources to help them improve. This might involve enrolling team members in training programs or courses, assigning them to work on projects that stretch their abilities, or pairing them with mentors or coaches who can provide guidance and support.

By taking the time to assess your team's strengths and weaknesses and develop their talent, you can create a more skilled and motivated workforce that is better equipped to meet your organization's goals and objectives.

Delegating effectively

Delegating effectively is a critical skill for any leader to develop. It involves assigning tasks to team members in a way that maximizes their strengths and abilities, while also allowing the leader to focus on their own responsibilities.

Effective delegation requires clear communication of goals and expectations, as well as trust in the team member's ability to complete the task. Leaders should begin by assessing the skills and expertise of their team members and identifying tasks that can be delegated to them. They should then communicate the task clearly, including expectations for quality, deadline, and any other relevant details.

It's important to remain available to provide support and answer any questions that may arise, but also to allow the team member the space to take ownership of the task and work independently. Finally, leaders should provide feedback and recognition for a job well done, reinforcing the value of the team member's contribution, and encouraging continued growth and development.

Here's an example. Sarah is a team leader at a marketing firm. She has a team of five members who have varying degrees of experience and expertise. Sarah understands the strengths and weaknesses of each member of her team and assigns tasks to them accordingly. She believes in delegating tasks to her team members to empower them and help them develop new skills.

One of Sarah's team members, John, has recently expressed interest in learning how to create social media ads. Sarah knows that John is talented in graphic design, but he has not had much experience with social media advertising. She decides to delegate a new project to him, which involves creating a social media ad campaign for a new product that the company is launching.

To help John with the project, Sarah provides him with clear guidelines and expectations, including the target audience, budget, and timeline. She also sets up regular check-ins to monitor his progress and provide feedback. Sarah knows that by delegating this project to John, he will have the opportunity to learn a new skill and develop his expertise. Additionally, the project will help him gain exposure to a new area of the business.

With Sarah's guidance and support, John completes the project on time and produces a high-quality social media ad campaign. Sarah's delegation allowed John to learn new skills, grow his confidence, and contribute to the company's success. Overall, Sarah's effective delegation allowed her team to perform at their best and achieve their goals.

Here are some techniques for delegating effectively:

1. Choose the right person: Before delegating a task, make sure that the person you're delegating to has the skills and knowledge needed to complete the task successfully.

2. Provide clear instructions: When delegating a task, be sure to provide clear and concise instructions. Be specific about what needs to be done, when it needs to be done, and how it should be done.

3. Set clear expectations: Be clear about the goals and objectives of the task, and what success looks like. Set realistic deadlines and milestones for the task.

4. Provide resources and support: Make sure the person you're delegating to has all the resources they need to complete the

task successfully. This may include access to information, training, and support.

5. Monitor progress: Check in regularly to see how the person is doing and offer support and guidance as needed. This will help ensure that the task is completed on time and to a high standard.

6. Provide feedback: After the task is completed, provide feedback to the person. Acknowledge their achievements and provide constructive feedback on areas where they can improve.

7. Encourage growth and development: Use delegation as an opportunity to help your team members grow and develop their skills. Provide opportunities for them to take on new challenges and responsibilities and offer training and support to help them succeed.

Effective delegation involves identifying tasks that can be assigned to others, communicating expectations clearly, and providing the necessary support and resources. By creating a culture of learning and growth, leaders can foster an environment where employees feel empowered to take ownership of their work and develop their skills.

Providing feedback and coaching for growth

Providing feedback and coaching for growth is an essential skill for leaders who want to develop and empower their team members. Effective feedback can help team members identify their strengths and areas for improvement, which can lead to personal and professional growth.

Coaching, on the other hand, involves working with team members to help them develop specific skills or achieve their goals. This requires leaders to have a deep understanding of their team members' strengths, weaknesses, and aspirations. It also involves the ability to provide constructive feedback and to help team members set realistic goals and develop action plans to achieve them.

Additionally, coaching involves providing ongoing support and guidance to team members, as well as celebrating their successes and recognizing their contributions to the team. Through effective feedback and coaching, leaders can help their team members reach their full potential and achieve their goals.

Although providing feedback and coaching for growth is a critical skill for leaders to develop to support the professional development of their team members. Not all feedback or coaching is good.

Good feedback is specific, timely, and focuses on behaviors rather than personal characteristics. It is also delivered in a way that is constructive and promotes growth rather than discouragement or shame. On the other hand, bad feedback can be vague, overly critical, or destructive. It can damage the relationship between the leader and team member, decrease motivation, and even lead to increased job dissatisfaction or turnover.

Therefore, it is essential for leaders to learn how to provide effective feedback and coaching that supports their team members' growth and development in a positive way.

Good example: Samantha is a sales manager who has noticed that one of her sales representatives, Jack, is not meeting his sales targets. Instead of immediately criticizing Jack, Samantha schedules a meeting with him to discuss his performance. During the meeting, Samantha shares specific data on Jack's sales performance, identifies areas where Jack could improve, and works with Jack to develop an action plan to help him meet his targets. Samantha also offers ongoing support and feedback to Jack as he works to improve his performance.

Bad example: Steve is a manager who has noticed that one of his employees, Sarah, is not meeting her performance goals. In a staff meeting, Steve publicly criticizes Sarah for her poor performance in front of the entire team, without offering any specific feedback or suggestions for improvement. Steve's approach humiliates Sarah and damages her motivation and self-confidence. As a result, Sarah becomes defensive and unresponsive to Steve's attempts to help her improve.

Here are some techniques for becoming better at providing feedback and coaching:

1. Be specific: When giving feedback, focus on specific behaviors or actions, rather than making general statements. This helps the person understand exactly what they need to improve.

2. Be timely: Try to provide feedback as soon as possible after the behavior or action you are addressing. This allows the person to remember the situation and the details of what happened.

3. Be constructive: Feedback should be delivered in a way that is constructive, rather than critical. Focus on what the person did well, as well as what they can improve on.

4. Be collaborative: Encourage the person to participate in the feedback process by asking them for their perspective and ideas for improvement. This helps to build trust and engagement.

5. Be consistent: Provide feedback and coaching on a regular basis, not just when something goes wrong. This helps to create a culture of continuous improvement.

6. Use the right tone: When giving feedback, use a tone that is respectful and empathetic. This helps the person feel safe and supported, which leads to greater receptiveness and willingness to improve.

By practicing these techniques, leaders can become more effective at providing feedback and coaching that helps their team members grow and develop.

Providing effective feedback and coaching is a crucial aspect of leadership. By taking the time to understand your team members' strengths and weaknesses, and providing constructive feedback and guidance, you can help them grow both personally and professionally. It is important to approach feedback in a positive and supportive manner, focusing on specific behaviors or actions that can be improved rather than criticizing the individual. By following the techniques outlined in this chapter and practicing effective communication, leaders can become more skilled at providing feedback and coaching, ultimately leading to a more productive and successful team.

Questions to Ponder

How do you identify and develop talent within your team?

What are some strategies for empowering team members to take on new challenges?

How do you balance the needs of the team with the needs of individual team members?

Chapter 6: Leading

Through Change and Adversity

"The only constant in life is change, and true leaders must navigate through it with grace and resilience."

When Lou Gerstner took over as CEO in 1993, IBM was struggling financially and had lost its position as a dominant player in the technology industry. Gerstner recognized that IBM needed to change to survive, and he implemented several strategies to turn the company around.

One of his key strategies was to focus on the customer, rather than on IBM's internal operations. He reorganized the company around customer segments, rather than around product lines, and implemented a more customer-centric approach to sales and marketing.

Gerstner also recognized the importance of technology in the changing marketplace and invested heavily in new areas such as e-commerce and data analytics. He also made the difficult decision to divest IBM's struggling PC business and focus on higher-growth areas.

Through these and other initiatives, Gerstner was able to turn IBM around and restore it to profitability. His leadership during this time is often cited as an example of successful change management in the business world.

As a leader, you must develop strategies to effectively guide your team through changes. The first step is to establish clear communication with your team, outlining the specific changes that are happening and why they are necessary. This helps to minimize confusion and resistance to the changes. Be sure to listen to your team's concerns and address them in a respectful and empathetic manner. Engaging in two-way communication ensures that everyone is on the same page and working towards the same goals.

Another important strategy for leading through change is to provide training and support to your team. New systems, processes, and tools can be daunting, so it's essential to provide resources and training to ensure your team is comfortable and confident with the changes. This can include offering one-on-one coaching or providing additional team training sessions. Regularly checking in with your team can help to identify areas where additional support is needed.

To minimize the stress and uncertainty that often comes with change, it's crucial to maintain a positive and optimistic outlook. Leaders who display a positive attitude and demonstrate confidence in the changes are better able to inspire their team and foster a sense of resilience. Regularly celebrating milestones and successes can help to maintain momentum and keep the team motivated.

Finally, it's important to recognize that change can be difficult, and setbacks are inevitable. As a leader, you must remain flexible and adaptable to changing circumstances. Be open to feedback and willing to adjust your strategies as needed. When setbacks do occur, use them as learning opportunities and encourage your team to do the same. By approaching change with a growth mindset, you can turn challenges into opportunities for growth and development.

Here is a list of activities that you can try with your team to better prepare for the changes that will come in your industry and organization.

One way to practice is through a role-playing exercise where team members take on different roles and respond to a hypothetical change in the organization. During the simulation, the leader can observe how team members react and respond and provide feedback on their performance. This can help the team become more comfortable with change and develop strategies for dealing with it in the future.

Another activity is to conduct a post-mortem analysis of a past change initiative. The leader can gather the team together and facilitate a discussion around a recent change that occurred in the organization. This can include discussing what worked well, what didn't work, and what could be done differently in the future. By reflecting on past experiences, the team can learn from their successes and failures, and be better prepared for future changes.

A third activity is to encourage team members to think about the potential impact of a change before it happens. This can be done through brainstorming sessions or individual reflections. By proactively considering the potential outcomes of a change, team members can prepare themselves and the organization for the change. This can also help to identify potential challenges and opportunities that may arise from the change.

Lastly, leaders can encourage team members to seek out opportunities for growth and development during times of change. This can be done through training sessions, mentoring, or job shadowing. By investing in the development of their team, leaders can ensure that team members are equipped with the skills and knowledge necessary to navigate changes successfully.

Managing conflict and difficult situations

As a leader, it is essential to know how to manage conflict and difficult situations that may arise in the workplace. These conflicts can occur between team members, departments, or even with external stakeholders, and if not handled appropriately, they can escalate and negatively impact productivity and morale. To effectively manage conflict, leaders should develop a set of strategies that allow them to address the issue at hand while maintaining positive relationships with all parties involved.

In 2014, Satya Nadella became the CEO of Microsoft, inheriting a company that was struggling to keep up with competitors in the mobile and cloud markets. He recognized that the company needed a significant cultural shift to achieve its goals and brought in his own leadership style to make it happen.

One of the key ways Nadella managed conflict was by shifting the company's focus away from internal competition and towards collaboration. He encouraged Microsoft's teams to work together across departments and to focus on the company's overall mission rather than individual goals. He also made it clear that he valued listening to the ideas and feedback of his employees, even if they disagreed with him.

Another step Nadella took was to change the company's culture from one of aggression and confrontation to one of empathy and compassion. He emphasized the importance of empathy and understanding the needs of Microsoft's customers and encouraged employees to focus on finding solutions to their problems. This helped to create a more positive and supportive work environment where employees felt valued and empowered to contribute to the company's success.

Nadella also recognized the importance of diversity and inclusion, both in terms of hiring practices and in creating a more open and accepting culture. He made it a priority to hire a diverse range of employees and to ensure that they felt included and supported at the company. He also encouraged open and honest communication about sensitive issues like race and gender, helping to build trust and understanding among his team.

Overall, Nadella's approach to managing conflict was focused on creating a positive and supportive work environment where employees felt valued, empowered, and encouraged to work together towards a common goal. By focusing on empathy, collaboration, and diversity, he was able to shift the company's culture and achieve success in the highly competitive tech industry.

One effective strategy for managing conflict is to remain calm and composed when dealing with a difficult situation. Emotions can run high during conflict, and it's essential to keep a level head to avoid making things worse. Leaders can practice deep breathing exercises, take a short break to gather their thoughts, or even seek the advice of a mentor or coach to help them manage their emotions.

Another strategy for managing conflict is to listen actively to all parties involved. Listening with empathy and an open mind can help leaders understand each person's perspective and the root cause of the conflict.

Leaders should ask open-ended questions and encourage all parties to share their thoughts and feelings. By doing so, they can identify the underlying issues and work towards a resolution that satisfies everyone's needs.

Leaders should also strive to find common ground and work towards a mutually beneficial solution. This can be achieved by focusing on shared goals and interests, rather than individual wants and needs. Leaders can facilitate discussions and brainstorming sessions to find creative solutions that meet everyone's needs. It's important to remember that compromise is necessary in most conflict situations and that leaders should be prepared to make concessions to reach a resolution.

Finally, leaders should follow up after a conflict has been resolved to ensure that the resolution is working and that everyone involved is satisfied. They should continue to monitor the situation and adjust as needed. Following up also shows that leaders care about their team members' well-being and are committed to maintaining positive relationships within the workplace.

In short, managing conflict and difficult situations is a crucial aspect of effective leadership. Leaders can manage conflict by remaining calm and composed, listening actively, finding common ground, and following up after a resolution has been reached. By doing so, they can maintain positive relationships within the workplace and ensure that productivity and morale remain high.

Overcoming obstacles and adversity

Bethany Hamilton, a professional surfer from Hawaii. In 2003, at the age of 13, she was attacked by a shark while surfing, resulting in the loss of her left arm. This could have been the end of her career, but instead, Bethany refused to let it hold her back. Just a few months after the attack, she was back in the water and eventually returned to professional competition.

To overcome the challenges of surfing with only one arm, Bethany had to adapt her technique and use a custom-made surfboard with a handle on the side. She also had to overcome the fear of getting back in the water after the traumatic experience. With hard work, determination, and support from her family and friends, Bethany was able to not only return to surfing but also achieve great success in her career.

Bethany's story is a powerful example of how perseverance and determination can help us overcome even the most challenging obstacles. She could have easily given up on her dreams after losing her arm, but instead, she found a way to adapt and thrive in the face of adversity. Her story has inspired many people around the world to never give up, no matter what challenges they may face.

Overcoming obstacles and adversity is an inevitable part of any leadership role. Leaders often face challenges that can range from minor setbacks to major crises. It is important for leaders to develop the ability to overcome obstacles and adversity effectively. One of the key strategies is to maintain a positive attitude. A positive attitude helps leaders to stay focused on finding solutions rather than getting bogged down by the challenges. This can be done by focusing on the opportunities that the situation presents rather than the negative aspects.

Another effective strategy for overcoming obstacles and adversity is to develop a clear plan. A clear plan helps leaders to understand the steps required to address the challenge effectively. It is important to break down the challenge into smaller, manageable tasks to avoid feeling overwhelmed. By creating a clear plan, leaders can take a systematic approach to tackling the challenge.

Leaders can also overcome obstacles and adversity by being adaptable. Adaptability is essential because situations can change quickly, and leaders must be able to adjust their plans accordingly. Leaders who are adaptable are better able to respond to new information, change direction when necessary, and find new ways to solve problems. They are also more resilient in the face of unexpected challenges.

Finally, leaders can overcome obstacles and adversity by building a strong support network. A support network can provide guidance, encouragement, and advice when facing challenges. This network can include colleagues, mentors, family members, or friends. It is important for leaders to build relationships with people who have experience in the areas where they need support. This can help leaders to gain valuable insights and perspectives and receive the emotional support needed to overcome the challenge.

Overcoming obstacles and adversity is an essential skill for any leader. Leaders who maintain a positive attitude, develop a clear plan, remain adaptable, and build a strong support network are better equipped to navigate challenges and emerge stronger on the other side. While it is impossible to predict every challenge that may arise, these strategies provide a foundation for overcoming obstacles and achieving success as a leader.

Questions to Ponder

How do you lead through change and adversity?

What are some strategies for maintaining your own resilience and staying positive during difficult times?

How do you help your team navigate change and uncertainty?

Chapter 7:

Continuous Improvement and Learning

"Achieving excellence is a journey, not a destination."

The healthcare company, Kaiser Permanente is committed to providing the highest quality healthcare services to its patients, and it recognizes that this requires ongoing learning and development by its employees.

To achieve this, Kaiser Permanente invests in a wide range of training and development programs for its employees, including courses on healthcare technology, patient care, and leadership skills. The company also encourages its employees to pursue advanced degrees and certifications, and it provides financial assistance to support these efforts.

Kaiser Permanente also has a strong focus on continuous improvement in its operations and processes. The company regularly reviews its practices and procedures to identify areas for improvement, and it engages its employees in these efforts through various feedback channels and improvement initiatives. This allows the company to continuously improve the quality of its services and outcomes for patients.

The commitment to continuous improvement and learning has allowed Kaiser Permanente to remain at the forefront of healthcare innovation and to consistently deliver high-quality care to its patients. It has also helped the company to attract and retain top talent in the healthcare industry, as employees are motivated by the opportunities for growth and development that the company provides.

Embracing a growth mindset as a leader

As a leader, embracing a growth mindset is essential to fostering personal and professional development within oneself and one's team. A growth mindset involves acknowledging that intelligence and abilities can be developed through dedication and hard work. With a growth mindset, leaders are open to learning and willing to take risks, as they recognize that failure is an opportunity for growth rather than a sign of weakness.

One way to embrace a growth mindset is to seek out new challenges and opportunities for learning. Leaders can take on projects that push them outside of their comfort zones, allowing them to develop new skills and perspectives. Additionally, seeking out mentors or coaches can provide valuable guidance and feedback that can facilitate personal and professional growth.

Another aspect of embracing a growth mindset is cultivating a culture of continuous learning within one's team. This can involve providing resources and opportunities for team members to expand their knowledge and skills, as well as encouraging open communication and feedback to promote learning and improvement.

Leaders who embrace a growth mindset also recognize the value of resilience in the face of setbacks and challenges. Rather than becoming discouraged or giving up, they view obstacles as opportunities for growth and learning. By reframing challenges in this way, leaders can develop a sense of resilience that can help them persevere through difficult times and come out stronger on the other side.

In summary, embracing a growth mindset is a crucial component of effective leadership. By committing to continuous learning and development, seeking out challenges and opportunities for growth, fostering a culture of continuous learning within one's team, and cultivating resilience in the face of obstacles, leaders can create an environment that supports personal and professional growth and development.

Under the leadership of Satya Nadella, Microsoft has shifted its culture from a fixed mindset to a growth mindset. Nadella encourages his employees to embrace a growth mindset by fostering a learning culture within the organization. He has introduced programs such as "One Week" and "Hackathons" to encourage employees to experiment and learn from their failures.

In addition, Nadella has also implemented changes in the company's performance review system to encourage growth and development. The company has shifted from a "stack ranking" system to a more collaborative and developmental approach to performance evaluations. This change allows employees to receive more feedback and support for their growth and development.

Identifying areas for personal and professional growth

Identifying areas for personal and professional growth is an essential component of leadership development. It involves recognizing areas in which a leader can improve and developing strategies to address these weaknesses. One effective method of identifying growth areas is to conduct a self-assessment, as we did in previous chapters. By reflecting on one's strengths and weaknesses and analyzing past successes and failures, a leader can gain insights into areas that require improvement.

Another strategy for identifying growth areas is to solicit feedback from others. Feedback from peers, subordinates, and superiors can be valuable in identifying areas for improvement. Constructive criticism can help a leader identify blind spots and areas that they may have overlooked. Additionally, feedback from others can provide insight into how a leader's behavior is perceived and how it affects others.

Once a leader has identified areas for growth, the next step is to develop a plan to address these weaknesses. The plan should be specific, measurable, achievable, relevant, and time-bound (SMART). It should outline the steps that a leader will take to achieve their growth objectives, including the resources required, timelines, and metrics for tracking progress. The plan should also identify potential obstacles and strategies for overcoming them.

Finally, it is essential to commit to ongoing learning and development. Growth is a continuous process, and leaders must remain committed to developing their skills and knowledge throughout their careers. This can involve pursuing formal education, attending conferences and workshops, reading books and articles, and seeking mentorship and coaching. By embracing a growth mindset and committing to ongoing learning, leaders can continue to improve their performance and achieve their full potential.

Identifying areas for personal and professional growth is a critical component of leadership development. Leaders should conduct self-assessments, seek feedback from others, develop SMART plans to address weaknesses, and commit to ongoing learning and development. By embracing a growth mindset and committing to continuous improvement, leaders can maximize their potential and achieve success in their careers.

For instance, a leader may recognize that they need to improve their public speaking skills to effectively communicate with their team or to represent their organization at events. To address this area for growth, the leader could enroll in a public speaking course or seek out a mentor who is experienced in public speaking to provide guidance and feedback. They may also look for opportunities to practice their skills, such as volunteering to give presentations at work or attending networking events where they can practice their communication skills.

Another example could be a leader recognizing that they need to improve their time management skills. They may find themselves constantly feeling overwhelmed and unable to effectively prioritize tasks, which can lead to missed deadlines and poor performance. To address this area for growth, the leader could research time management strategies and tools, such as time blocking or task prioritization methods. They may also seek out training or coaching to help them develop more effective time management habits and learn how to delegate tasks to their team to free up more of their own time.

A leader may also identify a need to improve their ability to provide feedback and coaching to their team members. Perhaps they have noticed that their feedback is often not well-received or that they struggle to effectively coach their team members toward growth and development. To address this area for growth, the leader could seek out training or coaching on effective feedback and coaching techniques. They may also look for opportunities to practice giving feedback and coaching, such as setting up regular check-ins with team members to discuss their progress and offer guidance.

Finally, a leader may recognize a need to improve their technical skills in a specific area related to their work. For example, they may need to improve their understanding of financial statements to better manage the financial performance of their team or organization. To address this area for growth, the leader could enroll in a course on financial statement analysis or seek out a mentor who is experienced in financial management. They may also look for opportunities to practice their skills, such as working on a project that requires financial analysis and presenting their findings to their team or organization.

Creating a culture of learning and development within your team or organization

Creating a culture of learning and development within your team or organization is critical to continuous improvement and growth. When team members are encouraged and supported in their pursuit of knowledge and skills, they become more engaged, motivated, and productive. As a leader, it's your responsibility to foster this culture and provide opportunities for learning and development.

One way to create a culture of learning is to provide regular training and development opportunities. This can take the form of workshops, seminars, online courses, or on-the-job training. By investing in your team's skills and knowledge, you're investing in the success of your organization.

Another way to create a culture of learning is to encourage feedback and reflection. Create a safe space for team members to share their thoughts and ideas, and encourage them to reflect on their experiences and learnings. By making reflection a regular part of your team's culture, you can help them identify areas for improvement and growth.

You can also create a culture of learning by modeling it yourself. As a leader, it's important to demonstrate a commitment to learning and development. Share your own experiences with your team and let them see how you apply what you learn to your work. By leading by example, you can inspire your team to do the same.

Finally, make learning and development a part of your team's goals and performance evaluations. Encourage your team members to set goals for their personal and professional growth and support them in achieving those goals. By making learning and development a priority, you can create a culture that values growth and continuous improvement.

One example is offering regular training and development opportunities to employees. For instance, a company could provide in-house training sessions, workshops, or seminars that focus on various skills and knowledge areas that are relevant to the employees' roles and the company's goals. Additionally, the organization could also provide access to online courses, webinars, or conferences that help employees stay up to date with the latest trends and practices in their industry.

Another example is providing opportunities for employees to take on new challenges and projects that allow them to develop new skills and gain experience. This can include assigning stretch assignments, giving employees opportunities to work on cross-functional teams, or encouraging employees to take on leadership roles in projects or initiatives. By providing these growth opportunities, employees can enhance their skills and build their confidence, which can ultimately benefit the organization.

Creating a culture of learning and development also involves promoting continuous feedback and coaching to employees. By providing regular feedback on their performance, employees can identify areas for improvement and receive guidance on how to enhance their skills and reach their goals. Coaching sessions can also help employees to better understand their strengths and weaknesses, develop action plans to address their development areas, and receive ongoing support and encouragement from their leaders.

Creating a culture of learning and development within an organization is crucial for fostering employee engagement, motivation, and retention.

By investing in employees' growth and development, organizations can also develop a competitive advantage by having a highly skilled and adaptable workforce that can respond to changing business needs and drive innovation.

Questions to Ponder

What is your approach to continuous learning and development as a leader?

How do you identify areas for personal and professional growth?

What are some strategies for creating a culture of learning within your team or organization?

Wrap Up and Final Words

Throughout this book, we have explored several critical aspects of effective leadership. One of the key takeaways is that great leaders inspire their teams to achieve remarkable things, by creating a positive and supportive work environment, identifying, and developing talent within their team, delegating effectively, providing feedback, and coaching for growth, leading through change, managing conflict and difficult situations, and embracing a growth mindset.

Creating a positive and supportive work environment is critical to a leader's success, as it promotes collaboration, engagement, and innovation. Developing talent within the team requires a leader to identify and nurture employees' skills, knowledge, and potential, which helps in building a more capable team. Effective delegation helps distribute tasks, reduces workload, and empowers team members to take ownership and accountability for their work.

Providing feedback and coaching for growth is essential to improve team performance, productivity, and employee satisfaction. Leaders should learn to lead through change, as it is inevitable in the modern business world. They should also be adept at managing conflict and difficult situations, as it is essential for maintaining team cohesion, trust, and respect.

Embracing a growth mindset is critical for leaders to continually improve themselves and their team. Leaders should identify areas for personal and professional growth, seek feedback, and actively pursue learning and development opportunities. Finally, creating a culture of learning and development within the team or organization is key to ensuring that employees are continuously growing and contributing to the company's success.

There are many stories of how leadership development has transformed companies and their success, but one inspiring example is that of General Electric (GE). In the early 2000s, GE was struggling to maintain its position as an industry leader, and its stock price was plummeting. Its CEO, Jack Welch, realized that the company needed to reinvent itself to survive.

Welch knew that the key to turning the company around was developing its leadership. He started a leadership development program called Crotonville, which aimed to create a culture of learning and development within the organization. The program was designed to identify and develop high-potential employees, and it focused on teaching leadership skills such as communication, decision-making, and strategic thinking.

The results of the program were remarkable. GE's leadership became more diverse, with more women and minorities in top positions. The company's performance improved, with revenue increasing by 20% and profits increasing by 80% over five years. Welch's successor, Jeff Immelt, continued the leadership development program and expanded it to include more employees.

The success of GE's leadership development program is a testament to the power of investing in the growth and development of employees. By creating a culture of learning and development, GE was able to attract and retain top talent, develop a diverse leadership team, and ultimately transform the company's performance. It's an inspiring example for any organization looking to improve its leadership and achieve success.

In conclusion, developing leadership skills is a continuous process that requires dedication, effort, and commitment. Through the chapters, we have learned the importance of effective communication, building relationships, motivating teams, managing change, and embracing a growth mindset. As a leader, it is essential to continuously identify areas for personal and professional growth, provide feedback and coaching for growth, and create a culture of learning and development within your team or organization. It is also important to remember that leadership is not about titles or positions but rather about the impact you make on others and the organization.

Leadership skills can be developed and honed over time through practice, feedback, and reflection. As you continue to develop your leadership skills, remember to stay curious, seek feedback, and be open to learning new things. Be intentional in your efforts to grow and develop as a leader and strive to create a positive and supportive work environment for your team.

Finally, I encourage you to continue learning and growing as a leader. Whether you attend leadership workshops, read books on leadership, or seek out a mentor, there are endless opportunities to continue developing your skills. Embrace the challenges that come your way and stay committed to your goals. Remember, great leaders are not born but made through dedication, hard work, and a willingness to learn and grow.

Questions to Ponder

What are some key takeaways from this book that you can apply to your own leadership style?

What are some areas where you can continue to grow and develop as a leader?

How can you use what you've learned to have a positive impact on your team or organization?

The Leader's Pledge

As a leader, I am committed to continuously developing myself and my team. I recognize that leadership is not just about having the right skills and knowledge, but also about continuously learning and adapting to change. Therefore, I will always be open to feedback and actively seek opportunities for growth and development.

I will encourage my team to take on new challenges, try different approaches, and learn from both successes and failures. I will provide opportunities for training and development, both through formal programs and on-the-job learning.

I will also make a conscious effort to stay up to date with the latest trends and best practices in my industry, attending conferences, networking with peers, and reading industry publications. I will seek out mentors and coaches who can provide guidance and support as I continue to grow and develop as a leader.

Most importantly, I will model the behavior I expect from my team. I will embrace a growth mindset, be open to feedback, and act on the areas where I need to improve. I will lead by example and inspire others to do the same.

here are some additional resources for leaders:

1. Harvard Business Review - This publication provides a wealth of articles, research studies, and case studies on leadership, management, and business strategy.

2. TED Talks - TED Talks cover a wide range of topics, including leadership, creativity, innovation, and personal development. Many of the talks are given by renowned leaders and experts in their fields.

3. LinkedIn Learning - LinkedIn Learning offers a variety of online courses on leadership, management, and professional development. These courses are taught by industry experts and cover a wide range of topics.

4. The Leadership Challenge by James M. Kouzes and Barry Z. Posner - This book is a classic on leadership and provides a framework for developing leadership skills.

5. The 7 Habits of Highly Effective People by Stephen R. Covey - This book provides practical advice on personal and professional development, including leadership skills.

6. The Lean Startup by Eric Ries - This book provides a framework for building and growing businesses through continuous innovation and experimentation.

7. The Art of Possibility by Rosamund Stone Zander and Benjamin Zander - This book provides a new perspective on leadership and personal development, encouraging readers to embrace possibility and creativity.

These resources can be a great starting point for leaders looking to continue their professional development and grow their leadership skills.